PREFACE

Who truly knows MATLAB, loves it! Who rejects MATLAB, doesn't know it!

MATLAB is the most universal engineering program existing today. An extract from the existing toolboxes (libraries) points out the wide range of applications: Aerospace Toolbox, Bioinformatics Toolbox, Communications Toolbox, Control System Toolbox, Filter Design Toolbox, Neural Network Toolbox, Optimization Toolbox, Partial Differential Equation Toolbox, Simulink, Statistics Toolbox, System Identification Toolbox, Fuzzy Logic Toolbox, Image Processing Toolbox...

Not only in the original engineering sciences MATLAB is an established program but also through other disciplines (for example applications like Financial Toolbox or Fixed-Income Toolbox) MATLAB has found wide acceptance and acknowledgement. These finance toolboxes mentioned above are now available in a new version, probably due to the financial crisis in 2008.

Wikipedia (as of November 2012, German version) writes about MATLAB :

„MATLAB (commonly written in capital letters) is a commercial, platform-independent software developed by MathWorks Inc. that allows solving mathematical problems and graphically visualizes the results. MATLAB is primarily set up as a program for numerical calculations by using matrices – therefore its name MAtrix LABoratory."

Google generated 65 million hits for the term „MATLAB". That is just five times less than the term „women" would generate, which shows the widespread usage of MATLAB.

There is an uncountable number of books on MATLAB. Just on www.amazon.com you would find more than 5.000 books. What makes this book different from other books about MATLAB?

Most books on MATLAB are engineering or mathematical books. They deal with a specific and complex problem of engineering sciences or numerical mathematics and demonstrate how to solve it with MATLAB. Even an experienced engineer would usually find these problems to be so complex and specific that she or he would understand them only after thorough analysing and studying – if at all. Only scientists and engineers with expertise in this subject could work with these books.

For engineering students with little knowledge in this specific matter, there is no adequate book for learning the basics about MATLAB.

Through this book it is possible to learn about MATLAB as an autodidact along with easy examples. The focus lies on learning about the software without any previous knowledge necessary.

The book consists of two parts:

In the first part MATLAB is explained in general. The „Help" function and how to get assistance as well, variables, operators, number formats and numbers including vectors and matrices are explained to start with. Then it shows how to create simple graphics and how to label them. The M-File and related functions are described in detail and explained through examples. Programming structures such as loops and comparisons make the end of the theoretical part. Each chapter ends with short exercises, to directly apply the content. The first part is appropriate and suitable for beginners – no matter what subject area or disciplines the student might come from – for the autodidact learning on MATLAB.

In the second part of this book, there is a number of exercises. The exercises are taken from the disciplines physics, mathematics and electrical engineering on a second semester university level and directed at students in electrical engineering.

To round off a collection of commands with the most important MATLAB commands an index is added at the end of the book.

This book was developed during my teaching at the university of applied sciences, „Fachhochschule Nordwestschweiz", Switzerland.

Niederlenz, February 2014   Stefan Wicki

1st edition February 2014

Further information available on: www.wictronic.ch

Proofreading: Marcel Merk, Silvia Schöning und Mirjam Wicki

Content: Peter Dähler und Silvia Schöning

Translated: Patric West, Marcel Merk, Dianna Tartoni

Printed and published by Books on Demand GmbH, Norderstedt

ISBN: 978-3-7357-8474-2

CONTENTS

1. HELP, HELP!

Commands: `help, lookfor`

1.1 Direct requests for assistance (`help`)

MATLAB offers several very good tools to get help. The simplest and most efficient way is to use the Command Window. For example to get help about the command `plot`:

Type the following on the Command Window:

```
help plot
```

This will give you the following result:

```
plot    Linear plot.
    plot(X,Y) plots vector Y versus vector X. If X or Y is a matrix,
    then the vector is plotted versus the rows or columns of the matrix,
    whichever line up.  If X is a scalar and Y is a vector, disconnected
    line objects are created and plotted as discrete points vertically at
    X.
... and so on
```

The following structure of the help listings applies:

- The most important is shown at the beginning (in the first paragraph). This information enables you to use the command. In the following paragraphs additional information for extended use is available.

- Please consider the `See also` part at the end of the support section about references to related commands:

```
See also plottools, semilogx, semilogy, loglog, plotyy, plot3, grid,
    title, xlabel, ylabel, axis, axes, hold, legend, subplot, scatter.
```

1.2 Indirect help request (`lookfor`)

If you do not know yet what command you want to use. Either you will use a MATLAB command collection or you'll use the `lookfor` command. This searches all the commands to a specific tag. E.g. you want to label a graphic and you don't know the command to do so.

Type the following on the Command Window:

```
lookfor annotation
```

This gives you the following results:

```
text                          - Text annotation.
annotation                    - creates an annotation object
scribecursors                 - Figure Pointers for annotations and plotedit.
startscribeobject             - Initialize insertion of annotation.
startscribepinning            - Turn annotation pinning mode on or off.
annotationddg                 - Dynamic dialog for Simulink Annotation type
objects.
getCallbackAnnotation         -
getCurrentAnnotation          -
getSelectedAnnotations        - Returns all selected annotations in the given
system
hdfan                         - MATLAB gateway to HDF multifile annotation
interface.
render_sptscribebtns          - Render the annotation portion of a toolbar.
```

The command `text` matches your needs the best. More detailed help is available by typing `help text`.

The search using the command `lookfor` can be interrupted anytime by typing CTRL+C.

1.3   Window based Help functions

Introduced in Version 6. MATLAB offers built-in window based help documentation known from other programs too. In MATLAB this help is clearly and well structured.

Help can be accessed through Help → MATLAB Help (or F1). The figure below shows the help documentation for the command `legend`.

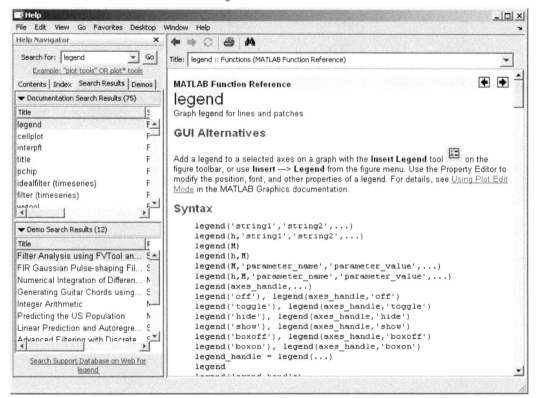

The window based help function can be accessed directly from the Command Window. Windows help for the command `legend` you can find by typing `doc legend` on the command line.

1.4 Short exercises for chapter one

- Study the help of the function `plot`.

- Look for help about the sinus function.

- Open the window based help documentation for the command `plot` and compare this help with the help text on the Command Window.

2. VARIABLES, OPERATIONS, NUMBER FORMATS

Commands: `+, -, *, /, format, whos, who, clear, clc`

2.1 The Command Window

The Command Window of MATLAB can be used as a calculator. MATLAB knows the basic operators `+, -, *, /`, and also constants `pi` and `j / i`. The result is shown directly on the bottom of the Command Window: the Command Line.

Example: You want to calculate the cross section of a wire with a diameter of 0.5mm. The cross section is:

```
0.5e-3^2*pi/4                    %¹e-3=10⁻³
```

You get the following result in the Command Window:
```
ans =
   1.9635e-007
```

It is more elegant to assign the diameter to a variable:

```
d=0.5e-3
```

You get:
```
d =
   5.0000e-004
```

Now calculate the area:

```
A=d^2*pi/4
```

You will get:
```
A =
   1.9635e-007
```

---

[1] The `%`-character declares a comment

If you find the output of the result to be too inaccurate, you can improve it using the `format` command.

```
format long

A

A =
     1.963495408493621e-007
```

The diameter is stored with the variable **d**, the area in the variable **A**.

You want to know all the variables stored on the Workspace. `whos` will provide you with a detailed list of these variables:

```
whos

  Name        Size                  Bytes  Class

  A           1x1                       8  double array
  ans         1x1                       8  double array
  d           1x1                       8  double array
```

while `who` is the smaller version thereof:

```
who

Your variables are:

A    ans    d
```

The variables on the Workspace appear in the „Workspace" window too and may also be edited.

With `save` „**desired file name**" the Workspace is saved in a binary file with the name „**desired file name**".

All variables in the Workspace can be deleted through the command `clear`. `clc` clears all previous inputs and outputs in the Command Window and will give you a clear screen.

2.2 Short exercises for chapter two

- Study the commands `clear` and `format`.

- Delete all variables in the Workspace. Clear the Command Window. Set the format for numbers back to its original accuracy.

- Calculate the weight of an aluminium plate with a diameter $d = 60$ mm and a thickness $t = 3$ mm. The specific weight of aluminium is 2700 kg/m^3.

3. NUMBERS, ARRAYS (VECTORS) UND MATRICES

Commands: `:`, `[1 2 3]`, `[1; 2; 3]`, `linspace`, `logspace`, `+`, `-`, `.*`, `*`, `./`, `/`

3.1 Manual Matrix Definition

In MATLAB each variable is treated as a matrix. We define the variable **a** to be a number **5**.

```
a=5

a =
     5
```

The matrix size is beeing examined.

```
whos

  Name      Size                 Bytes  Class

  a         1x1                      8  double array
```

The variable **a** is defined as 1x1matrix with one element. This element has got the value of **5**.

We define the vector **b** (one-dimensional matrix).

```
b=[1, 2, 3]

b =
     1     2     3
```

The matrix size is being checked out.

```
whos

  Name      Size                 Bytes  Class

  a         1x1                      8  double array
  b         1x3                     24  double array
```

The variable **b** is defined as 1x3 matrix with three elements. These elements have the value of **1**, **2** and **3**. Such a (one-dimensional) matrix is called row vector or array.

We define a complete matrix **c**.

```
c=[1, 2, 3; 4, 5, 6]

c =
      1      2      3
      4      5      6
```

This is equivalent to

```
c=[[1, 2, 3],
   [4, 5, 6]]

c =
      1      2      3
      4      5      6
```

The matrix size is checked.

```
whos
```

Name	Size		Bytes	Class
a	1x1		8	double array
b	1x3		24	double array
c	2x3		48	double array

The variable **c** is defined as 2x3 matrix (two rows, three columns) with six elements.

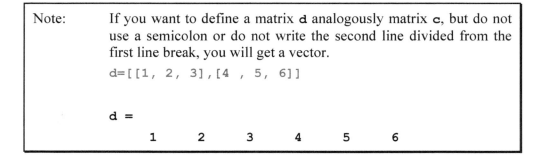

Note: If you want to define a matrix **d** analogously matrix **c**, but do not use a semicolon or do not write the second line divided from the first line break, you will get a vector.

```
d=[[1, 2, 3],[4 , 5, 6]]

d =
      1     2     3     4     5     6
```

3.2 Automatic Matrix Definition

Often you will want to define vectors with equally spaced integers.
Example: Definition of a vector with ten elements from 1 to 10.

```
e=1:10

e =

    1    2    3    4    5    6    7    8    9   10
```

If you want to define a vector with fractional values that all show the same spacing between the elements you use `linspace`.

```
f=linspace(0,2*pi,6)

f =
        0    1.2566    2.5133    3.7699    5.0265    6.2832
```

If you want to define a vector with fractional value elements that show logarithmic spacing between these elements you use the `logspace` command.

```
g=logspace(-1,1,6)

g =
    0.1000    0.2512    0.6310    1.5849    3.9811   10.0000
```

For a row vector defined through ones only, we use the command `ones`.

```
h=ones(1,10)

h =
    1    1    1    1    1    1    1    1    1    1
```

The same applies to the command `zeros`.

3.3 Stacking of elements and vectors

Elements, vectors or even whole matrices can be stacked to form new ones.
Here examples with the variables defined above.

```
A=[a,b]

A =
     5     1     2     3
```

```
Note:        MATLAB distinguishes between capitals and lower case letters. E.g.
             A and a  are totally different variables!
```

```
B=[d;f]

B =
    1.0000    2.0000    3.0000    4.0000    5.0000    6.0000
         0    1.2566    2.5133    3.7699    5.0265    6.2832
```

3.4 Access to matrix elements

The general syntax for accessing individual elements is:

```
Variable name(row, column)
```

Based on the variable **c** we will take a look at how to access the matrix elements.

```
c =
     1     2     3
     4     5     6
```

We would like to know the value of the matrix element in the first row third column:

```
c(1,3)

ans =
     3
```

Analogously, if we want to know the value in the second row and first column it is:

```
c(2,1)

ans =
      4
```

A special case is the access to vector elements. The third element of the vector **f** is as follows:

```
f(3)

ans =
      2.5133
```

> Note: MATLAB starts counting the matrix elements with **1**. Taking **0** as an index is not allowed:
>
> ```
> f(0)
> ```
>
> ```
> ??? Subscript indices must either be real positive
> integers or logicals.
> ```

It is also possible to access several elements of a vector. Vectors may be limited, e.g. in measurements with a row of numbers to delete the invalid measurements:

```
e(3:end)

ans =
      3      4      5      6      7      8      9      10
```

3.5 Vector calculation and matrix calculation

We define two new vectors **m** and **n** of the same length:

```
m=1:6

m =
     1     2     3     4     5     6


n=2:2:12

n =
     2     4     6     8    10    12
```

We add the two vectors:

```
E=m+n

E =
     3     6     9    12    15    18
```

We subtract the two vectors:

```
F=m-n

F =
    -1    -2    -3    -4    -5    -6
```

Now we want to multiply both vectors, element by element:

```
M=m.*n

M =
     2     8    18    32    50    72
```

> Note: Without the Point Operator MATLAB wants to apply matrix opera-
>   tions.
>
>
>   m*n
>
>
>   ??? Error using ==> *
>   Inner matrix dimensions must agree.

To obtain the scalar product of the two vectors, one needs to transpose the second vector:

```
N=m*n'

N =
    182
```

By transposing the first vector, one obtains the matrix product of the two vectors m' and n:

```
O=m'*n

O =
     2     4     6     8    10    12
     4     8    12    16    20    24
     6    12    18    24    30    36
     8    16    24    32    40    48
    10    20    30    40    50    60
    12    24    36    48    60    72
```

The same applies to division:

```
P=m./n

P =

    0.5000    0.5000    0.5000    0.5000    0.5000    0.5000


Q=m/n

Q =
    0.5000
```

3.6 Short exercises for chapter three

- Study the commands `linspace` and `logspace`. What are the differences?
- Create a vector **a** with 20 elements from 0 to 19 (without `linspace`).
- Create a vector **b** consisting of 20 elements from 0 to 2π.
- Create a 2x20 Matrix **A** with the vectors **a** and **b**.
- Set the last two elements in the last column to 0.

4. Two-dimensional Grahps

Commands: `plot, subplot, grid on/off, axis, hold on/off, title, xlabel, ylabel, legend`

This part of the theory is explained using a graph of a sine function and a cosine function.

4.1 Representation in one axis (`plot`)

An x-vector from 0 to 4π with 200 values is generated:

```
x=linspace(0,4*pi,200);
```

> Note: A semicolon at the end of a command (or a calculation) suppresses the output on the command window.

The corresponding y-vector is calculated:

```
y=sin(x);
```

The z-values are calculated:

```
z=cos(x);
```

The first figure is being opened:

```
figure(1);                     %or simply figure
```

With the first use of `plot` a new figure is created automatically. The command `figure` then is not necessary. For reusing `plot` again, one draws into the current figure. If one wants to create a new figure, the command `figure` must be executed.

1. The sine function is drawn:

```
plot(x,y);
```

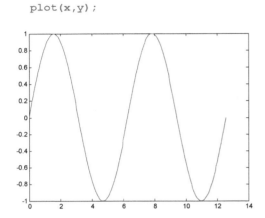

2. The axes are being set:

```
axis([0 4*pi -1 1])
```

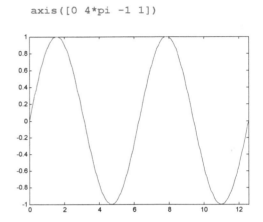

3. The grid is turned on:

```
grid on
```

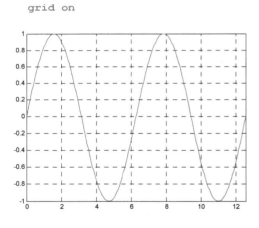

4. A title fixed:

```
title('sine function')
```

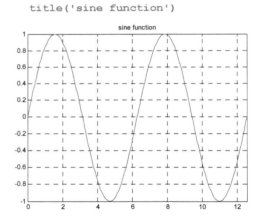

5. The x-axis is being labeled:

```
xlabel('angle [rad]')
```

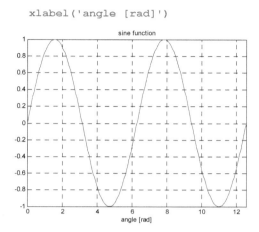

6. The cosine function is drawn with red dashed line:

```
hold on, plot(x,z,'r--')
```

7. The title is changed:

```
title('sine- and cosine function')
```

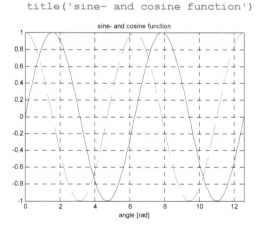

8. A legend added:

```
legend('sine','cosine')
```

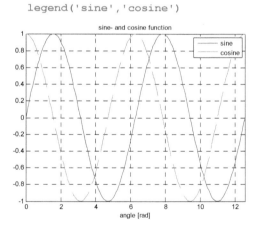

Notes and comments:

- In case the command `plot(x,y)` is used, the vectors **x** and **y** must have the same length.

- The command `plot(y)` can be used for a fast check of the vectors. The **x**-axis shows as the index of the **y**-vector.

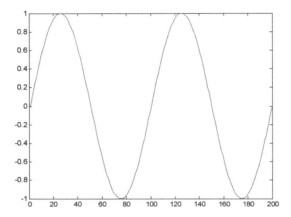

- The command `hold on`, causes, that multiple graphs can be drawn in one figure (on an axis). If you do not use this command as in the example above, the sine curve is deleted and only the cosine curve is shown. The command `hold on` can be turned off again by `hold off`.

- Strings are marked with single quotes e.g. `title('sine- and cosine function')`.

4.2 Display of several plots in a figure (`subplot`)

The `subplot` command allows the arrangement of several plots in one figure. The *first digit* of the `subplot` shows how many *rows* the window should be divided, whereas the *second digit* shows how many *columns* the window should be divided into. The *last digit* is a serial number and will be used to address the specific drawing.

1st example `subplot(12x)`:

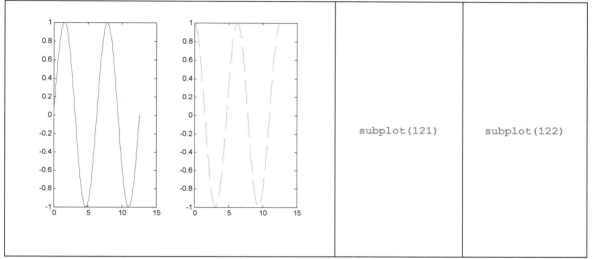

2nd example `subplot(32x)`:

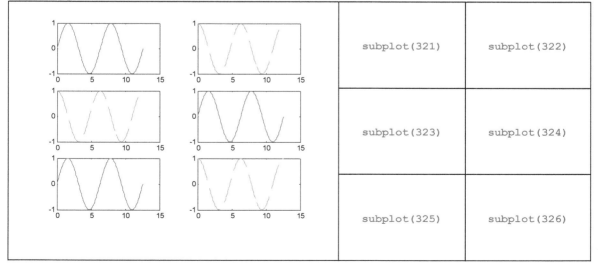

In this example, the sine and the cosine function are shown in two axes. The variables **x**, **y**, and **z** are used as defined in the previous chapter.

A second figure is opened (this is required so the first figure may not be overwritten):

```
figure(2);                          %or simply figure
```

1. The sine function is shown in the first row:

```
subplot(211), plot(x,y);
```

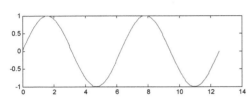

2. The axis is set:

```
axis([0 4*pi -1 1])
```

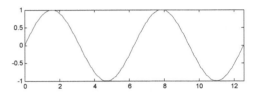

3. The grid is turned on:

```
grid on
```

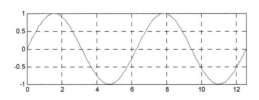

4. A title is given:

```
title('sine function')
```

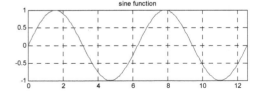

5. The cosine function is drawn in the second row red and dashed:

```
subplot(212), plot(x,z,'r--')
```

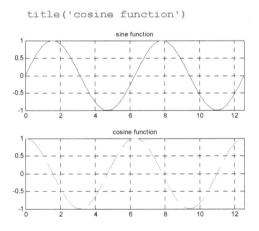

6. Axis and grid must be set separately:

```
axis([0 4*pi -1 1]), grid on
```

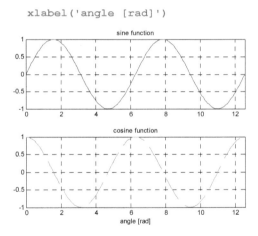

7. The title is given:

```
title('cosine function')
```

8. The x-axis is named:

```
xlabel('angle [rad]')
```

9. With `subplot` you can change between the axes:

```
subplot(211),                        subplot(212),
title('The sine function is above')  title('The cosine function is
                                     below')
```

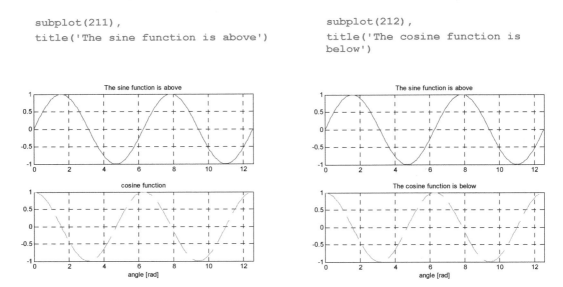

The individual plots can be placed anywhere in the window.

4.3 Short exercises for chapter four

- Plot sin(x), sin($2x$) and sin($3x$) together in one figure. Label this figure in detail (axes) and create a legend.

- Plot these functions all underneath each other.

- Show e^x and ln(x) in one figure

5. The M-File, the Matlab-Editor

Commands: `*.m, clc, clear all, close all, path, addpath`

An M-File is a text-file (ASCII-file), which contains a series of individual MATLAB-commands. MATLAB also provides a powerful editor for these files. Searching for mistakes is considerably simplified!

5.1 The file name

> Important: Any file name can be chosen for the MATLAB M-Files. The ending thereof must be „.m". However if the name of the M-Files is the same as an already existing M-File (e.g. a MATLAB-function) MATLAB might not find the old function anymore.

Before a name is chosen it is important to check whether such a file name or such a function already exists. This can be done with `help` „**desired filename**".

> Tip: If you use names in languages other than English you will rarely have conflicts with any existing functions as MATLAB is programmed and written in English.

The file name *may not* contain the following characters (spaces and special characters):
`+, -, ., @, #, *, &, ?, !`

The file name *should not* contain the following characters (accents):
`ö, ä, ü, é, à, è`

The file name *may* contain the following characters, but numbers not as first character:
`_, 0, 1, 2, 3, ...,` (and all letters).

5.2 Structure of an M-File

The structure of an M-File is shown here based on the file `Mandelbrot.m`. The focus thereof is not on its *content* but on the *structure*!

The numbering of the subtitles in the text correlates with the numbered parts of the M-File `Mandelbrot.m` (to the left of the file).

5.2.1 The Header *(1-6)*

It makes sense starting off any M-File with a header describing the file and its functionality.

1. A comment starts with a `%`-character. All text after the `%` is considered as comment and will be highlighted in green.

2. In case there are self-written functions used in the M-File that do not derive from MATLAB itself, these functions are to be listed here. Troubleshooting and searching for mistakes from not working scripts is considerably simplified.

3. In case there are external files used in this script (e.g. data files) these are to be listed here too.

4. Does the M-File produce new files these are to be listed here.

5. Is the file meant to access global variables, these should be mentioned here. I advise not to use global variables generally – yet with large simulations they are inevitable.

6. The header will be listed as help text with the call `help Mandelbrot`. (see p. 26, where it's listed). The header ends by the first line in the M-File that does not start with a `%`-character (6).

```
1    %*********************************************************************
     % Project        : Draw the Mandelbrot set
     % Author         : Stefan Wicki
     % File name      : Mandelbrot.m
     % Beginning date : 03.10.12
     % End date       : 12.10.12
     % Version        : 1.0
     %*********************************************************************
     % A Mandelbrot set is known as a fractal set. Points (coordinates
     % in the complex plane) are iterated until they either converge or diverge.
     % How fast a point diverges (e.g. the amount of the complex number exceeds a
     % certain limit), is given by the colour of the same. Points near the centre
     % (0,0j) converge to a larger extent than points that are further out.
     % The algorithm is as follows (z is a complex number):
     % z(N+1) = z(N) + z(N)^2
     %*********************************************************************
     %
2    % used functions:     -
     %
3    % input files:        -
     %
4    % output files:       -
     %
     %*********************************************************************
     %
5    % global variables:   -
     %
     %*********************************************************************
6
```

```
help Mandelbrot
```

****

```
   Project          : Draw the Mandelbrot set
   Author           : Stefan Wicki
   File name        : Mandelbrot.m
   Beginning date   : 03.10.12
   End date         : 12.10.12
   Version          : 1.0
```

****

```
   A Mandelbrot set is known as a fractal set. Points (coordinates
   in the complex plane) are iterated until they either converge or diverge.
   How fast a point diverges (e.g. the amount of the complex number exceeds a
   certain limit), is given by the colour of the same. Points near the centre
   (0,0j) converge to a larger extent than points that are further out. The
   algorithm is as follows (z is a complex number):
   z(N+1) = z(N) + z(N)^2
```

****

```
   used functions:       -

   input files:          -

   output files:         -
```

****

```
   global variables:     -
```

****

5.2.2 *Initializations* (7-10)

7. Before new variables are defined, you should clean up the Workspace and delete variables from old programs.

> Note: If global variables (`global`) are used or inside functions, the command `clear all` in line (7) should be removed. Otherwise the global variables respectively the input arguments of the function will be deleted as well.

8. Now one starts with the initialization of variables, constants, matrices and vectors.

9. A description of the same eases the reading of M-Files, even if an M-File for example is already one year old.

10. Often initialized variables are used for creating base vectors and matrices for the rest of the program.

```
7    clc; clear all; close all; close all hidden;


     %-------------------------------------------------------------------
8    % Initializations:
     %-------------------------------------------------------------------


     % Definition of the area in the complex plane
9    Real_Min   =   -2;          %most negative point real part
     Real_Max   =   0.7;         %most positive point real part
     Imag_Min   =   -j;          %most negative imaginary point
     Imag_Max   =   j;           %most positive imaginary point

     N_Real     =   300;         %Number of points in x-direction (real)
     N_Imag     =   300;         %Number of points in y-direction (imag)

     LIMIT      =   1e6;         %Limit for diversion
     iter       =   30;          %Number of iterations


10   RE=linspace(Real_Min, Real_Max, N_Real);
     IM=linspace(Imag_Min, Imag_Max, N_Imag);
```

5.2.3 *Calculation and output* (11, 12)

11. Now one starts with the actual calculation.

12. Often results are displayed graphically.

```
%------------------------------------------------------------------------
% calculation of the Mandelbrot set:
%------------------------------------------------------------------------

x=RE;
y=imag(IM);
Z=zeros(N_Real,N_Imag);

for k=1:N_Real
    for m=1:N_Imag
        z=0;
        for n=1:iter
            z=z^2;
            z=z+RE(k)+IM(m);
            if abs(z)>LIMIT
                break
            end
        end
        Z(k,m)=n;
    end
  end

figure;
hold off;
contourf(x,y,Z');
axis off;


%------------------------------------------------------------------------
% END
%------------------------------------------------------------------------
```

5.3 Short exercises for chapter five

Repeat the short exercises in chapter four but save this code in a well commented M-File. Check with `help` „**your_filename**" the help to your file.

- Use the MATLAB editor and check it out. Test the functionality of the built-in debugger by setting breakpoints. For trial and error build in some mistakes in your code.

- Study the commands `path` and `addpath`. Add your first M-File to the search path. Use the pathbrowser.

6. Own Functions and Error Handling

Commands: `function, return, nargin, error`

A function is an M-File, which gets variables (vectors, matrices) assigned to. A function can also give output such as returning variables (but does not have to).

6.1 The name of the function

The naming of functions is analogical to the naming of M-Files:

> Important: The file name of a MATLAB function may be chosen arbitrarily. The extension must be „.m". However, if the name of the new MATLAB function is the same as an already existing function, this will be overwritten.

Again, we can check on existing functions with `help` „**desired function name**".

6.2 Construction of a function

The construction of a function is analogical to the construction of an M-File.

Therefore in this section only the additional definitions will be shown on the basis of the function `grad.m`.

The section numbers in the text correspond to the numbered parts of the function `grad.m` (to the left of the file).

6.2.1 Function definition

1. The function generally is defined as follows:

```
function [output argument 1, 2, ...] = function name(input argument 1, 2, ...)
```

In our example:

```
function [ux,uy] = grad(x,y,z)
```

A function may not have return values, but *usually has input arguments*. There are also functions with neither input nor output values, that use the local Workspace of a function (variables declared in a function are not known outside the function).

> Note: Function name and file name must be the same. Otherwise the function will not be recognized (1)! In our example:
>
> file name: `grad.m`
>
> → function definition: `function [ux,uy] = grad(x,y,z)`

```
%*********************************************************************
% Project        : Determines the gradient of a function of 2 variables (x, y)
% Author         : Stefan Wicki
% File name      : grad.m
% Beginning date : 10.02.11
% Ending date    : 10.02.11
% Version        : 1.0
%*********************************************************************
%
% function [ux,uy] = grad(x,y,z)
%
% ux  =   gradient in x-direction
% uy  =   gradient in y-direction
%
% x   =   vector with the x-coordinates
% y   =   vector with the y-coordinates
% z   =   matrix with the values
%
% the first two matrix arguments, must have length(x) = n and length(y) = m
% where [m,n] = size(z)
%
%*********************************************************************
%
% used functions:      -
```

```
  %
  % input files:        -
  %
  % output files:       -
  %
  %*******************************************************************************
  %
  % global variables:   -
  %
  %*******************************************************************************
```

```
1     function [ux,uy] = grad(x,y,z)
```

6.2.2 Access to input arguments

2. The input arguments (`x,y,z`) are known to the function when called up. They can be accessed normally.

Even if the values of arguments are changed inside the function, outside of the function the values remain the same.

6.2.3 Calculation of output values

3. The output values or return values (`ux,uy`) are calculated inside the function. When the function is exited the values are stored in the return values.

6.2.4 End of a function (exiting)

4. If nothing special is noted, a function ends with the last line of the executable code.

A function can be terminated earlier with the command `return`.

```
  %--------------------------------------------------------------------------
  % Calculates the gradient in x-direction:
  %--------------------------------------------------------------------------

  % The gradient is calculated by mutual displacement of the vectors
  % fx|y=(z2-z1)./(x2-x1)
2     for k=1:length(y)            % "cut" slices in x-direction
3         ux(k,:)=([z(k,:) 1]-[1 z(k,:)])./([x 1]-[1 x]);
      end

      % Eliminate edge effects
3     ux(:,1)=ux(:,2);
3     ux=ux(:,1:size(ux,2)-1);
```

```
%----------------------------------------------------------------
% Calculates the gradient in y-direction:
%----------------------------------------------------------------

% The gradient is calculated by mutual displacement of the vectors
% fy|x=(z2-z1)./(y2-y1)
for k=1:length(x)              % "cut" slices in y-direction
    uy(:,k)=(([z(:,k)' 0]-[0 z(:,k)'])./([y 1]-[1 y]))';
end

% Eliminate edge effects
uy(1,:)=uy(2,:);
uy=uy(1:size(uy,1)-1,:);

%----------------------------------------------------------------
% END
%----------------------------------------------------------------
```

2

3
3
4

6.3 Calling up a function

The general call of a function is:

```
[output value 1, 2, ...] = function name(input argument 1, 2, ...)
```

In our example:

```
[ux,uy] = grad(x,y,z)
```

thereof the following rules apply:

- For calling up a function the program *allows* us using other variable names too (e.g. `[A,B]=grad(r,s,t)`).

- If the function is called with no output arguments, even though it has got such, only the return value of the first output argument is returned to the Command Window.

- Also functions can be written that allow a variable number of input arguments (most MATLAB functions are in this way). Refer to `varargin` and `varargout`.

Note:	A function can be called only if it is also known to MATLAB!
	Therefore the function must be located in the current directory or the location of the file must be added to the MATLAB path (`addpath` or pathbrowser of MATLAB).

6.4 Short exercises to chapter six

- Write a function

  `function [add, sub, mult, div, pow] = dual(a, b)`

  which adds `(add)` the two numbers a and b, subtracts `(sub)`, multiplies `(mult)`, divides `(div)` and potentiates `(pow)`. Test this function thoroughly.

- Think about how and which error handling for this function could be useful and reasonable.

- Study the help to the MATLAB functions `return, nargin, nargout` and `error`.

7. LOOPS, BRANCHES AND COMPARISONS

Commands: `for, while, break, if, elseif, else, <, <=, >, >=, ==, ~=, &, |, ~`

7.1 Loops

There are two different commands for loop structures: `for` and `while`.

The `for`-command will be used for setting „*integer*" conditions and increase the indexes. The `while`-command is used if the command's instruction can be translated in the sense of „*as long as*" or „*while*".

The `for`-loop is used more frequently.

7.1.1 The `for`-loop

The general structure of a `for`-loop is as follows:

```
for variable = condition
     statements;
end
```

The example of a program calculating the squares of the numbers 1 to 10:

```
for k = 1:10
    x(1,k)= k;
    x(2,k)= k^2;
end
x
```
results in:
```
x =
```

1	2	3	4	5	6	7	8	9	10
1	4	9	16	25	36	49	64	81	100

Note:	The favourite index of most programmers is `i` and `j`. You may use this, but should not, since `i` and `j` in MATLAB are pre-defined as an imaginary unit!

7.1.2 The `while`-loop

The general structure of a `while`-loop is as follows:

```
Initializing;                   %Initializing of the conditional variables
while condition                 %as long as the condition is true...
      statements;
      change of the condition;
end
```

This program also gives us the square numbers from 1 to 10. Please consider the differences to the `for`-command:

```
k=1;                            %initializing of the conditional values
while k<=10                     %so long as k smaller or equal to 10
      x(1,k)= k;
      x(2,k)= k^2;
      k=k+1;                    %increase k by 1
end
x
```

The `while`-structure seems more complex, still it has its validity especially if conditions are set by *fractional* values – or if while entering a loop the number of iterations is unknown.

7.1.3 Early exit of loops (`break`)

By using the command `break` a loop can be left prematurely, e.g. before the condition is false.

If one has several nested loops, the command `break` causes the program to leave only the inner loop. If there still is an outer loop, this one will run normally.

7.2 Branches (flow control)

7.2.1 The `if`-branch

The `if`-command can be understood as an „if-then"-structure. The general structure of the `if`-command is as follows:

```
if condition1
      statements;
elseif condition2
      statements;
elseif condition3
      statements;
...
else
      statements;
end
```

If you have only one condition, this then simplifies the general structure to:

```
if condition1
      statements;
else
      statements;
end
```

The following program determines the algebraic sign of a number **a**:

```
if a<0
      disp('the number is negative')
elseif a==0
      disp('the number is zero')
else
      disp('the number is positive')
end
```

7.2.2 The `switch`-branch

The `switch`-command is used if the expected values of the input are known and have specific values. The general structure of the `switch`-command is:

```
switch variable              %variable to be analyzed
    case value1              %case1
        statements;
    case value2              %case2
        statements;
    ...
    otherwise                %case1 to case2 has not occurred
        statements;
end
```

The following program assigns the number **a** to a weekday (1→Monday, 2→Tuesday, ..., 7→Sunday):

```
switch a
    case 1
        disp('Monday')
    case 2
        disp('Tuesday')
    case 3
        disp('Wednesday')
    case 4
        disp('Thursday')
    case 5
        disp('Friday')
    case 6
        disp('Saturday')
    case 7
        disp('Sunday')
    otherwise
        disp('invalid input!')
end
```

7.3 Comparisons

7.3.1 *Simple comparisons / equations* $(<, <=, >, >=, ==, ~=)$

The condition in loops or branches often requires the comparison between values or expressions.

The relational operators are below:

<	less than
<=	less than or equal to
>	greater
>=	greater than or equal to
==	equal
~=	unequal

Note:	To test the variables **a** and **b** for equality the command **a==b** is used. Do not use **a=b**, otherwise **b** will be stored in **a**!

7.3.2 *Linking of comparisons, logical operators* $(\&, |, ~)$

If several logical comparisons are linked with each other, logical operators are used. They are summarized in the following table below:

&	AND
|	OR
~	NOT

The following program examines the codomain of the variable **a**:

```
if (a>5)&(a<10)
     'The number is in between 5 and 10'
elseif (a==5)|(a==10)
     'The number is 5 or 10'
else
     'The number is smaller than 5 or greater than 10'
end
```

7.4 Short exercises to chapter seven

- Write a function `function [dez] = hex2dez(hex)`, that changes a hexadecimal number (only one digit) `hex` into a decimal number `dez`.

- Also create an error handling for the same function.

8. EXERCISE AND PRACTICE

Exercise 1: Parabola

Introduction

The trajectory parabola represents the path of a ball that is thrown with a certain initial velocity and a certain launch angle.

The trajectory parabola can be expressed in the xy-coordinate plane:

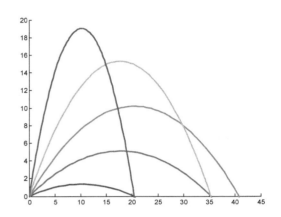

$$x(t) = |\vec{v}| \cdot \cos(\alpha) \cdot t$$

$$y(t) = |\vec{v}| \cdot \sin(\alpha) \cdot t - g \cdot \frac{t^2}{2}$$

$x(t)$:   x-components of the trajectory [m]

$y(t)$:   y-components of the trajectory [m]

$|\vec{v}|$:   initial velocity of the projectile [m/s]

α: launch angle [grad, rad]

t: time [s]

g: gravitational constant [9.81 m/s^2]

Task

Program an M-File with MATLAB that describes the parabola. It may be possible to alter the number of parabolas shown in the M-File. Which launch angle maximizes the distance in x-direction of the shot?

Helpful commands

linspace
figure
hold
axis
for
title
xlabel
ylabel
legend
num2str

Exercise 2: Impedance Matching

Introduction

We have a maximum power transfer when the load resistance R_L is the same as the source resistance R_q. The ratio of the power in the load resistance P_L to the available power P_{AV} can be described by the following formula:

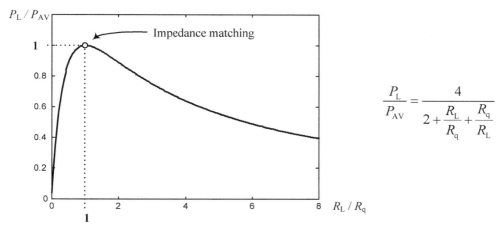

$$\frac{P_L}{P_{AV}} = \frac{4}{2 + \dfrac{R_L}{R_q} + \dfrac{R_q}{R_L}}$$

P_L / P_{AV} in function of R_L / R_q and impedance matching

Task

Visualize the above formula in MATLAB.

Show this graph in a linear, semi-logarithmic (x, y) and double-logarithmic plot.

Helpful commands

```
linspace
figure
plot
subplot
semilogx
semilogy
loglog
line
text
hold
title
xlabel
ylabel
legend
```

Exercise 3: Band-pass filter

Introduction

A band-pass filter is practical to eliminate certain frequencies of a signal. A band-pass filter can be realized using a resonant circuit.

Task

Show the output voltage for the illustrated network in the complex plane (as an animation!) in function of the frequency.

Use the command `compass`. Write your program so that the start and stop frequency are automatically adjusted to values of L and C.

Choose the input voltage to (1 +0·j) V.

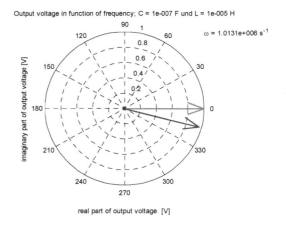

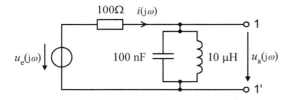

Helpful commands

```
linspace
for
compass
hold on
hold off
num2str
pause
title
xlabel
ylabel
text
```

Exercise 4: T-Network

Introduction

The given circuit consists of a source, a transfer element (T-structure) and a load. The load resistance varies in the range of $R_L = 0 \ldots \infty$.

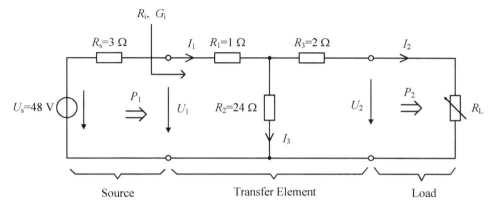

Task

We are looking for all currents and voltages in the network. The prepared table is to be calculated. Draw P_2 and η as a function of R_L.   ($\eta = P_2 / P_1$)

R_L [Ω]	R_i [Ω]	G_i [mS]	I_1 [A]	I_2 [A]	I_3 [A]	U_1 [V]	U_2 [V]	P_1 [W]	P_2 [W]	η [-]
0										
1										
6										
10										
14										
22										
38										
46										
70										
∞										

Helpful commands

```
[]
.*
./
disp
plot
hold
title
xlabel, ylabel
```

Exercise 5: One-Port

Introduction
On a one-port the following current and voltage is measured:

$u(t) = 2 \cdot \cos(10 \cdot t - \pi/3)$,

$i(t) = 3 \cdot \cos(10 \cdot t)$.

Task
Calculate the power $p(t)$ and sketch them, along with the current and voltage.
Calculate the average of the power P.

Helpful commands
```
linspace
.*
figure
plot
hold
title
xlabel
ylabel
legend
sum
```

Exercise 6: Lissajous Figure

Introduction

A Lissajous figure is formed by two harmonic signals, one plotted in the x- and the other in the y-direction of a coordinate system. One signal has an integer multiple frequency of the other. The Lissajous figure can be changed by changing the phase from one signal to the other.

Mathematically expressed:

$$x(t) = \sin(\omega_1 \cdot t)$$
$$y(t) = \sin(n \cdot \omega_1 \cdot t + \varphi)$$

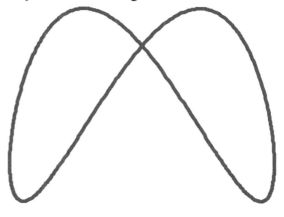

$x(t)$: x-component of the time signal [-]

$y(t)$: x-component of the time signal [-]

$\omega_1 =$ $2\pi f$: circle frequency [s^{-1}]

t: time [s]

n: natural number [1, 2, 3, ...]

φ: phase shift from x- to
y-signal [rad]

Task

Program an M-File in MATLAB which plots the Lissajous figure continuously. The frequency of the y-component is increased in steps (factor n), the phase should be continuously increased from 0 ° to 360 °. The presentation should be flicker-free and visually pleasing.

Helpful commands

```
linspace
figure
hold
axis
colordef
plot
pause
for
```

Exercise 7: Fourier synthesis

Introduction

Each periodic function can be described by a sum of cosine and sine waves (Fourier sequence):

$$u_{\text{per}}(t) = \underbrace{\frac{a_0}{2}}_{\text{DC-Value}} + \underbrace{\sum_{n=1}^{\infty} a_n \cdot \cos(n \cdot \omega t)}_{\text{cosine waves}} + \underbrace{\sum_{n=1}^{\infty} b_n \cdot \sin(n \cdot \omega t)}_{\text{sine waves}}$$

A square wave is described by the following sum:

$$u_{\text{rectangle}}(t) = \hat{U} \cdot \frac{4}{\pi} \cdot \left\{ \sin(\omega t) + \frac{1}{3}\sin(3\omega t) + \frac{1}{5}\sin(5\omega t) + ... \right\} = \hat{U} \cdot \frac{4}{\pi} \cdot \sum_{n=1,3,5,...}^{\infty} \frac{1}{n} \cdot \sin(n \cdot \omega t)$$

Task

a) Program an M-File, which composes a square wave by its Fourier series using the formula above.
    Plot the individual frequency components.

b) Write the function `function = fouriersynthesis (a,b)` which can synthesize any periodic time signal out of the vectors `a`, `b` (coefficients a_n und b_n). Plot the individual frequency components.

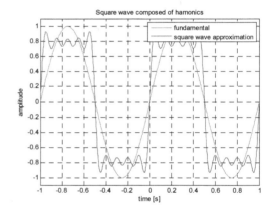

Helpful commands

```
linspace
figure
hold
plot3
stem
```

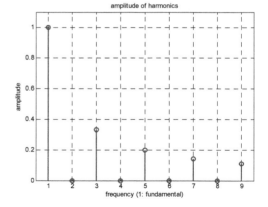

Exercise 8: RC-Circuit

Introduction

On the basis of this exercise it should be understood, how simulation tools such as PSPICE®
simulate circuits in the time domain. This is investigated using a simple RC element.

At the input is a time-dependent voltage source
$u_e(t)$. Using the values R and C the output voltage and the current through the resistor can be
calculated.

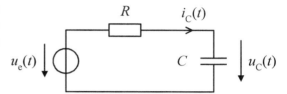

The current $i_C(t)$ through the resistor R is calculated using Ohm's law:

$$i_C(t) = \frac{u_e(t) - u_C(t)}{R}$$

This current flows into the capacitor and increases – when the direction of current is positive –
the voltage of the capacitor. The stored charge Q in the capacitor can be calculated in two
ways:

$$Q = C \cdot U_C \qquad \text{or} \qquad Q = \int_0^t i_C(t) \cdot dt + Q_0$$

For very small time steps ($\Delta t \ll \tau$) applies: $\Delta q = C \cdot \Delta u_C$ or $\Delta q = i_C(t) \cdot \Delta t$

These two equations can be equated to: $C \cdot \Delta u_C = i_C(t) \cdot \Delta t$

Rearranging the equation, one obtains a linearized equation for the change in voltage Δu on the
capacitor, that is valid for small time steps Δt ($\Delta t \ll \tau$). t_1 is Δt later than t_0.

$$\Delta u_C = \frac{i_C(t) \cdot \Delta t}{C} \qquad \rightarrow \qquad u_C(t_1) = u_C(t_0) + \underbrace{\frac{i_C(t_0) \cdot \Delta t}{C}}_{\Delta u_C}, \quad \text{for } \Delta t \ll \tau, \quad \Delta t = t_1 - t_0$$

Task

Program an M-File, which by the above algorithm calculates the charging curve of an RC element and compare it with the calculated exponential function. How big is the error in depend-
ence of $\Delta t / \tau$?

Exercise 9: Resonant circuit

Introduction

MATLAB is suitable for the calculation and representation frequency responses of linear networks.

Task

Plot the frequency response for $\underline{Z}$ between the terminals 1 and 1' of the circuit shown to the right (gain and phase).

Choose for the frequency response both a linear and logarithmic scale.

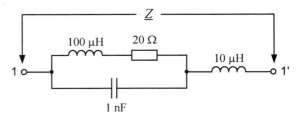

Helpful commands

linspace
logspace
abs
angle
axis
plot
subplot
semilogx
title
xlabel
ylabel
legend

Exercise 10:   Nonlinear Load

Introduction

A voltage source with $U_q = 4$ V and $R_q = 1$ Ω supplies a nonlinear resistor. The nonlinear resistor can be described by following characteristic:

$$U = -0.47 \cdot I^4 + 4.9 \cdot I^3 - 15 \cdot I^2 + 14.66 \cdot I$$

Task

Plot both characteristic lines in the range of $I = 0 \ldots 4$ A and determine the operating point.

Helpful commands

```
linspace
.^
.*
figure
plot
hold
title
xlabel
ylabel
legend
```

Exercise 11:   Sine-Approximation with Polynomials

Introduction

For the implementation of mathematical functions in a microprocessor or DSP, polynomial approximations or look-up table (LUT) can be used.

LUT with a good resolution requires a large memory space; the polynomial approximation on the contrary will take time for calculating.

For example, consider a sine function $y = \sin(x)$. In the interval $[-\pi/2, \pi/2]$ this function can be approximated very well by a polynomial function of the degree n, as it is steadily increasing:

$$y_{poly}(x) \cong \sin(x) \quad [-\tfrac{\pi}{2}, \tfrac{\pi}{2}]$$

It is difficult to determine the coefficients of the polynomial function. MATLAB does do that.

Mathematically, a polynomial approximation can be described as follows:

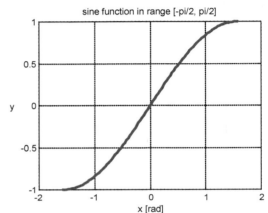
sine function in range [-pi/2, pi/2]

$$y_{poly}(x) = a_n \cdot x^n + a_{n-1} \cdot x^{n-1} + \ldots + a_1 \cdot x + a_0 \xrightarrow{\;e.g.\; n=3\;} a_3 \cdot x^3 + a_2 \cdot x^2 + a_1 \cdot x + a_0$$

$y_{poly}(x)$:   value of polynomial function

$a_n \ldots a_0$:   coefficient of the polynomial

Task

a)   Program an M-File in MATLAB which calculates the coefficients of the approximation above. The error of the approximation should be less than 1%.

b)   Program in MATLAB a function `function s = sinus(x)`, which can replace the Matlab function `sin`. Test this function extensively.

Helpful commands

```
polyfit
mod
polyval
subplot
length
if
```

Exercise 12:   **Tetra Pak**

Introduction

We have a cube where the ratio V/O of the volume V to the surface O is maximal (compared to other rectangular shapes). What about the Tetra Pak? Have the developers of the Tetra Pak considered something?

Therefore we examine one block with constant volume and varying length a and b. The length c results from the given volume V and length a and b.

From the resulting blocks, we analyze the surface O and the ratio volume to surface V/O.

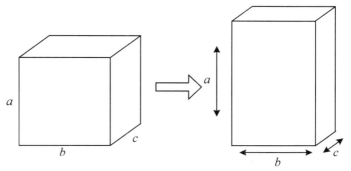

Task

Program an M-File to analyze the blocks. Visualize the ratio V/O as a function of the length a and b as a 3D-plot or contour plot.

Helpful commands

linspace
mesh
meshc
contour

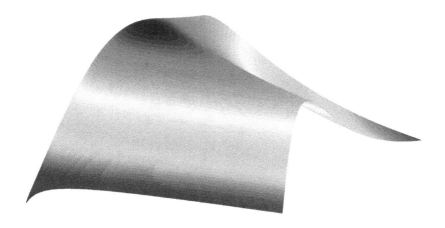

9. SUMMARY OF THE MOST IMPORTANT COMMANDS

GENERAL COMMANDS	
help	Display help text in Command Window
who	List current variables in Command Window
size	Size of array
length	Length of vector
clear	Clear variables and functions from memory
^C	Terminates the execution
exit, quit, ^Q	exit from MATLAB

MATRIX-	VECTOR-	OPERATIONS
+	+	Addition
–	–	Subtraction
*	.*	Multiplication (Matrix, Array)
/	./	Right division (Matrix, Array)
\	.\	Left division (Matrix, Array)
^	.^	Power (Matrix, Array)
'	'	Conjugate a Matrix, transpose a vector
.'		Transpose a matrix

MATRIX-MANIPULATION	
rot90	Rotate matrix 90°
fliplr	Mirror/flip matrix on a vertical axis (left/right)
flipud	Flip a matrix on the horizontal axis (up/down)
tril	Extract lower triangular part of a matrix
triu	Extract upper triangular part of a matrix
:	Access to individual rows or columns of a matrix

SPECIAL MATRICES AND VECTORS	
diag	Diagonal matrices and diagonals of a matrix
eye	Identity matrix
ones	Ones array: Matrix filled with „1"
zeros	Zeros array: Matrix filled with „0"
linspace	Linearly spaced vector
logspace	Logarithmically spaced vector
rand	Uniformly distributed pseudorandom numbers

COMPARISONS	
<	Less than
<=	Less than or equal to
>	Greater than
>=	Greater than or equal to
==	Equal
~=	Not equal
&	Logical AND
|	Logical OR
~	Logical NOT

SPECIAL SIGNS	
.	Decimal point
...	Continuation: continue command on the next line
,	Separation of function arguments
;	Output suppression, line end
%	Start of Comment
:	Vector generating

MATLAB CONSTANTS	
ans	Default variable for unassigned function values.
eps	Spacing of floating point numbers: smallest number in MATLAB: accuracy of floating point arithmetic
pi	π, 3.1416...
i, j	Imaginary unit, $\sqrt{-1}$
inf	Infinity
NaN	Not-a-Number
clock	Current date and time as date vector
date	Current date as date string
nargin	Number of function input arguments
nargout	Number of function output arguments

PROGRAM STRUCTURES	
if	Conditionally execute statements
elseif	used with `if`; `if` statement condition
else	used with `if`
end	Terminate scope of `for`, `while`, `switch`, `try`, and `if` statements
for	Repeat statements a specific number of times
while	Repeat statements an indefinite number of times
break	Terminate execution of `while` or `for` loop
return	Return to invoking function
pause	Wait for user response
pause(n)	pauses for n seconds before continuing

PROGRAMMING AND M-FILES	
input	Prompt for user input
error	Display message and abort function
function	Add new function
eval	Execute string with MATLAB expression
global	Define global variable

TEXT UND STRING	
abs	Returns the ASCII value of a string
num2str	Convert numbers to a string
int2str	Convert integer to a string
strcmp	Compare strings
hex2num	Converts a HEX-string into a number

COMMAND WINDOW	
clc	Clear Command Window
home	Send the cursor home (back to the top)
disp	Displays the array, without printing the array name
echo	Display statements during function execution

GRAPHICS	
plot	Linear plot
loglog	Log-log scale plot
semilogx	Semi-log scale plot: logarithmic x-axis, y-axis linear
semilogy	Semi-log scale plot: logarithmic y-axis, x-axis linear
polar	Polar coordinate plot
mesh	3D mesh surface plot
contour	3D contour plot
bar	Bar graph
hist	Histogram: bar graph for distributions (statistics)
errorbar	Error bar plot

LABELING OF GRAPHICS	
title	title of a figure (Graph title)
xlabel	X-axis label
ylabel	Y-axis label
grid on	Adds major grid lines to the current axes
text	Text annotation: labeling of the graph, placement by coordinates
gtext	Text annotation: labeling of the graph, placement by mouse click
ginput	Output of xy coordinates through mouse click

FIGURES AND AXES	
axis	Control axis scaling and appearance
hold on	Hold current graph: plot will not be overwritten
shg	Show graph window: brings the current figure in the foreground
clf	Clear current figure
subplot	Create axes in tiled positions
print	Print figure or model. Save to disk as image or file

BASIC CALCULATIONS	
abs	Absolute value
angle	Phase angle
sqrt	Square root
real	Complex real part
imag	Complex imaginary part
conj	Complex conjugate
round	Round towards nearest integer (up or down)
fix	Round towards zero (nearest integer)
floor	Round towards minus infinity (nearest integer)
ceil	Round towards plus infinity (nearest integer)
sign	Signum function. Sign of a number $+ / - / 0$
rem	Remainder after division
exp	Exponential e^x
log	Natural logarithm (ln)
log10	Common (base 10) logarithm (log)

TRIGONOMETRIC FUNCTIONS	
sin	Sine of argument in radians
cos	Cosine of argument in radians
tan	Tangent of argument in radians
asin	Inverse sine, result in radians
acos	Inverse cosine, result in radians
atan	Inverse tangent, result in radians
sind	Sine of argument in degrees
cosd	Cosine of argument in degrees
tand	Tangent of argument in degrees
asind	Inverse sine, result in degrees
acosd	Inverse cosine, result in degrees
atand	Inverse tangent, result in degrees

POLYNOMIALS	
`poly`	Convert roots to polynomial
`roots`	Find polynomial roots
`polyval`	Evaluate polynomial
`conv`	Polynomial multiplication
`deconv`	Polynomial division
`residue`	Partial-fraction expansion (residues)
`polyfit`	Fit polynomial to data

VECTOR ANALYSATION	
`max`	Largest component (maximal value)
`min`	Smallest component (minimal value)
`mean`	Average or mean value
`median`	Median value
`std`	Standard deviation
`sort`	Sort in ascending or descending order
`sum`	Sum of elements
`prod`	Product of elements
`cumsum`	Cumulative sum of elements (discrete integration)
`cumprod`	Cumulative product of elements
`hist`	Histogram
`corrcoef`	Correlation coefficients

INTERPOLATION	
`spline`	Cubic spline data interpolation
`intrp1`	1-D interpolation (table lookup)
`Interp2`	2-D interpolation (table lookup)
`polyfit`	Fit polynomial to data

10. INDEX

www.ingramcontent.com/pod-product-compliance
Lightning Source LLC
LaVergne TN
LVHW080119070326
832902LV00015B/2667